CW00401178

A BOOT UP

THE WHITE PEAK

Roger Redfern

First published in Great Britain in 2011

British Library Cataloguing-in-Publication Data
A CIP record for this title is available from the British Library

ISBN 978 1 906887 16 2

PiXZ Books
Halsgrove House, Ryelands Industrial Estate,
Bagley Road, Wellington, Somerset TA21 9PZ
Tel: 01823 653777
Fax: 01823 216796
email: sales@halsgrove.com

An imprint of Halstar Ltd, part of the Halsgrove group of companies
Information on all Halsgrove titles is available at: www.halsgrove.com

Printed and bound in China by Toppan Leefung Printing Ltd

Contents

How to use this book 4

1 **High above Lower Dovedale** 7

2 **The length of Lathkill Dale** 13

3 **An Alstonefield round** 19

4 **Taddington and Chelmorton** 25

5 **Sharp summits above the
Upper Dove** 31

6 **Longstone Edge and Coombs Dale** 37

7 **Peak Forest, Eldon Hole and
and Eldon Hill** 43

8 **Villages at the limestone edge** 49

9 **Parsley Hay, Pilsbury Castle and
Carder Low** 55

10 **Wetton and Thor's Cave** 59

How to use this book

The White Peak is the name given to the ancient heart of the Peak District National Park, where the Carboniferous limestone lies exposed on the surface and the younger Millstone Grit has been worn away by weathering in its various forms. The area offers walking of varying standards from easy to challenging, all in attractive upland landscapes.

The core of the White Peak rises to lesser altitude than parts of the surrounding Millstone Grit but some of its more pronounced hilltops reach respectable heights — like Eldon Hill which attains 1,541 feet (470 metres) west of Castleton. The limestone plateau is dissected by beautiful and sinuous dales, some of them dry where their streams run underground.

Fascinating routes, short and longer, can be created using one or other of the attractive villages that punctuate this district as the start and finish point. Each route here is graded from Easy to More Challenging with further details of distance, height ascended and the type of terrain covered, so helping the reader to choose a suitable route. The information blocks contain details of distances and heights in both imperial and metric measures.

All the walks are covered by Ordnance Survey Outdoor Leisure Map 24 — "The Peak District — White Peak area" except for the northern part of Walk 7, where you will need to refer to the southern edge of OS Outdoor Leisure Map 1 — "The Peak District — Dark Peak area".

The maps in this book give only outlines of each route. Reference to the OS map will add interest and help avoid going astray.

Always go well equipped, especially on the routes that involve tougher terrain and higher altitude. If unsure of fitness try one of the easier routes first! Not all the routes described have convenient places providing refreshment so always take some food and drink.

Tell someone where you are going and your expected time of return. And, having checked the weather forecast, only tackle the more demanding routes in clear conditions.

Useful websites:

Peak District National Park
www.peakdistrict.gov.uk

Railway travel
www.nationalrail.co.uk

Bus travel
www.transpeak.co.uk

Peak District Tourist Board
www.visitpeakdistrict.com

Peak & Northern Footpaths Society
www.peakand northern.org.uk

Five Wells chambered cairn, near Taddington.

Key to Symbols Used

Level of difficulty:

Easy

Moderate

More Challenging

Map symbols:

	Park & start
	Tarred Road
	Footpath
	Walk Footpath
	River, stream or brook
■	Building
+	Church
▲	Triangulation pillar or other landmark
	WC
	Refreshments
🍺	Pub

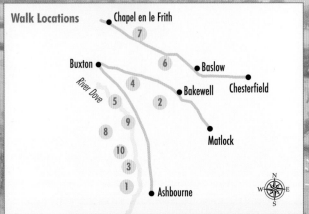

Walk Locations

Chapel en le Frith

7

Buxton

6

Baslow

River Dove

4

2

Bakewell

Chesterfield

5

9

8

Matlock

10

3

1

Ashbourne

N
W   E
S

6

High above Lower Dovedale

Far above the dale-bottom crowds.

The deep limestone gorge cut by the middle reaches of the River Dove on its way from Axe Edge to the River Trent is one of the most popular parts of the White Peak. Not so well known are the high ridge tops to either side. The crest of the high ground that lies west of Dovedale makes a particularly interesting route, giving fresher air and broader vistas than are experienced walking beside the river in the shady dale bottom.

The most dramatic part comes on the traverse of Bunster Hill's summit at 1,079 feet (329 metres) followed by its rocky south-east ridge with ever

Level: 🐾 🐾
Length: 6 miles (9.5 kms)
Ascent: 1,050 feet (320 metres)
Terrain: Field paths; dry valley; steep, wooded slopes; rocky ridge and descent.
Park & Start: Stanshope hamlet. GR 127542
Info: Information centre at Ilam Hall. GR 132507. Refreshments at Isaac Walton Hotel and Ilam Hall (National Trust).

closer views across the mouth of Dovedale to the conical peak of Thorpe Cloud. The steep descent over scree and through thorn thickets leads to gentler walking across the fields to the estate village of Ilam before fairly easy walking by fields or Ilam Moor Lane and so back to the start at Stanshope hamlet.

Over the Dove, Dovedale.

1 From Stanshope hamlet walk a short way east down Pasture Lane then take the field path heading south-east that soon brings us down the steep-sided Hall Dale.

2 When we reach Dovedale bottom go right and follow the west bank of the delightful Dove as far as the dramatic limestone cliff called Ilam Rock.

3 At the foot of Ilam Rock turn up the fiercely steep, wooded slope on the right to eventually gain the top of the wood (Dovedale Wood) and so aim left (south) along the upper edge of the wood.

4 The path turns right (west) to pass the appropriately named Air Cottage. Terrific views of Dovedale.

Looking across Dovedale from Air Cottage.

The limestone gorge of Dovedale (the River Dove marks the boundary between Derbyshire and Staffordshire for its entire course) has been popular with tourists for three centuries. The early visitors were fascinated by its spectacular limestone rock architecture and the beauty of its silent river which became famous as a trout stream for sporting anglers like Charles Cotton and Isaac Walton.

High above Lower Dovedale

On Bunster Hill looking to Thorpe Cloud.

5 Immediately after Air Cottage do not continue west on the obvious track but strike across towards the south, keeping to the edge of the wood that marks the top of the big slope overlooking Dovedale.

6 Reach the 1,079 feet (329 metres) top of Bunster Hill and go over the stile which brings you out onto the sharp, stony crest of this hill's south-east crest. Continue to the end of the ridge overlooking the mouth of Dovedale with the conical profile of Thorpe Cloud directly opposite.

7 Take care now on the steep and broken descent to the south, aiming through thorn trees towards the weir on the River Dove just upstream of the public car park.

8 Walk the very short distance down the public road and opposite the car park (on the left beside the river) take the footpath to the right which crosses two fields before passing behind the Isaac Walton Hotel. Then head west across three fields.

In the last hundred years or so large areas of Dovedale have developed all enveloping woods which have tended to hide much of those grand spires and turrets of limestone. In recent times there have been efforts to remove some of this offending tree cover.

Thorpe Cloud from the slopes of Bunster Hill.

(9) Either take the path heading north just where there's a stile onto the public road at the entrance to Ilam village and so continue below the steep slopes of Bunster Hill and where a path crosses take the left one to reach Ilam Moor Lane. Or walk through Ilam village, heading north along Ilam Moor Lane.

(10) Walk north along Ilam Moor Lane to the starting point at Stanshope.

Bunster Hill (left) and Thorpe Cloud with Ilam church.

Note: At Damgate it is possible to avoid the final section of road walking by following a field path to the right.

2 **The length of Lathkill Dale**

Exploring one of the White Peak's loveliest dales.

No less an authority than the great Charles Cotton used the character of "Piscator" to state that the River Lathkill was "by many degrees the purest and most transparent stream" that he ever saw, at home or abroad, and bred "the reddest and best Trouts in England".

Truly that great authority on the history and scenery of the district

J.B.Firth described Lathkill Dale in 1905 "among the fairest of the Derbyshire dales." Walking through this limestone valley these days brings just as much joy as it did a century ago.

Walking up or down this deep dale may give the impression of a sheltered, verdant landscape but we don't easily see the exposed limestone

Level: 🥾 🥾
Length: 6.75 miles (10.5 kms)
Ascent: 525 feet (160 metres)
Terrain: Field paths, riverside paths and some short, steep sections.
Park & Start: Youlgreave village centre.
GR 210642
Info: Refreshments at Youlgreave.

plateau through which the river has cut its way through millennia. To north and south lie the upland farmlands of Over Haddon and Youlgreave parishes respectively. To give a flavour of what was once called "this blasted heath" the second part of our route climbs out of the valley to traverse the drystone wall territory of what was once medieval monastic farmland.

Over Haddon
Meadow Place Grange
River Lathkill
Cales Dale
Ash ge
Limestone Way
Back Lane
Moor Lane
Youlgreave

13

Youlgreave village from Back Lane.

1 Leave the village of Youlgreave near the post office and youth hostel to walk north along Moor Lane for a very short distance and take the footpath (right) that crosses the many small fields that are remnants of the enclosed lands of the earlier medieval manorial three-field system.

2 Reaching Back Lane turn right and almost immediately turn left to follow the path going north to Meadow Place Grange.

3 Cross the field behind Meadow Place Grange to the edge of the wood and go steeply down to cross the River Lathkill by the footbridge.

Youlgreave parish church is one of the largest in the Peak District. The parish register contains remarkable entries for "the great snow" of the winter of 1614–15 when "four feet of snow lay upon the playne" from 16th January to late March. Thereafter came "the great drought" when no rain fell from 25th March until 2nd May and then only three showers fell until 4th August "so that the greater part of the land was entirely burnt up".

Meadow Place Grange.

The path to Meadow Place Grange.

The various granges that lie upon the limestone plateau here – like Meadow Place Grange and One Ash Grange – are remnants of the outlying farms owned and run by the various medieval religious houses. One Ash, for instance, was given by the new Norman overlords to the Cistercian monks of Roche Abbey in what is now South Yorkshire. It was great sheep country and eventually passed to the Cavendish family at Chatsworth, to which it still belongs.

4 Turn left and so follow the north bank of the river for two miles (3.25 kms) to the footbridge at the mouth of Cales Dale.

(5) Use the footbridge to cross to the south side and climb up lower Cales Dale to join the Limestone Way Long Distance Footpath.

(6) Turn left and climb out of Cales Dale to follow the Limestone Way across the open fields of the plateau, heading south-east for almost 1.5 miles (2.5 kms) to reach Back Lane at a road junction. On this last section we reach about 1,023 feet (312 metres), highest point of our route.

(7) Cross Back Lane and go down Moor Lane and very soon the Limestone Way turns off to the right. We, though, continue down Moor Lane to enter Youlgreave at the place where we started earlier.

Over Haddon from Back Lane.

The Eastern Edges from near Meadow Place.

The Limestone Way above Cales Dale.

3 An Alstonefield round

A contrasting walk over little trodden territory before reaching the more popular ground of the middle Dove Valley.

Level: 🐾 🐾
Length: 5.5 miles (8.5 kms)
Ascent: 500 feet (150 metres)
Terrain: Some lane and tracks, upland pastures and riverside paths. One stiff pull up from the River Dove.
Park & Start: Alstonefield village. GR 131556
Info: Inn at Alstonefield.

The pretty village of Alstonefield sits quite high on its plateau about 880 feet (270 metres) above sea level but it doesn't feel at all exposed to the elements. There are trees aplenty about the church and little village green. It may have lost its post office, shop and café but there's still an inn.

Walking off to the north we come to wilder, open ground and soon begin the descent into Narrowdale. This dry valley is overlooked by Narrowdale Hill and Gratton Hill and in winter is known locally as the place that "gets no sun". The twin farms in Narrowdale have seen better days but still boast the largest Shorthorn cattle herd in this country. You will see many of the multi-coloured beasts roaming free range over these steep slopes throughout the year.

Later we come down to the foot of beautiful Beresford Dale, where the

River Dove is tree-bowered and famous as one of the finest stretches of trout stream in the country, forever associated with Charles Cotton and Isaac Walton and the latter's classic *The Compleat Angler*, first published in 1653. Continuing southwards beside the Dove we enter the wilder, stonier Wolfscote Dale before escaping westwards up the fierce dale-side to cross fields back to our starting point.

① Set out from the middle of Alstonefield, along the lane heading north for about ⅔ mile (1 km). At a slight leftward bend approaching a small wood take the footpath on the right which aims due north through stone-walled fields.

② Cross a walled track at right angles and head towards Narrowdale Hill, soon beginning the descending traverse with the dry valley of Narrowdale below on the right.

③ We soon see the trees and roofs at Narrowdale Farm immediately below and ahead. Go through a gate into the yard between the two old farmhouses and then turn right.

Cottages at Alstonefield.

This part of the Dove Valley is forever associated with that pair of seventeenth century anglers, Charles Cotton and Isaac Walton. Cotton's lovely Fishing Temple stands at the northern mouth of Beresford Dale (somewhat upstream of that part of the valley this walk covers) and is not accessible to view. In winter, though, it can be espied through the leafless trees from the public path to Hartington. Its pyramidal roof and lattice windows give it the countenance of something from a fairy tale.

In the village, Alstonefield.

On the path to Narrowdale.

4 Follow the track for about 0.75 mile (1.25 km). Keep left where a path cuts off to the right.

Looking north over Narrowdale, late winter.

By the beginning of the nineteenth century Cotton's Fishing Temple had become "much dilapidated" but a century later it had been restored, and so remains to this day. A tangible link with the golden age of fly fishing in this "queen of silver trout streams".

(5) On reaching the lower end of Beresford Lane turn right and soon cross the River Dove on the footbridge.

(6) Walk south-east across the level riverside pasture, noting the caves in the lofty crag to the left. Continue alongside the left bank of the river right down Wolfscote Dale.

(7) In about 1.3 miles (2 kms), soon after passing the mouth of Biggin Dale (on left), look out for the river crossing.

Narrowdale and Narrowdale Hill.

8 Cross the Dove and follow the steep path up this western slope of the dale to eventually come out onto the open fields of the plateau and head across them.

9 On reaching the walled track turn left (south) and soon get to the public road (Lode Lane) where we turn right along it to soon gain Alstonefield village.

Summer in Wolfscote Dale.

4 Taddington and Chelmorton

A plateau route linking two high-set villages.

It was fortunate for Taddington village that it was by-passed by the A6 trunk road (Bakewell to Buxton section) before the last war. Its narrow main street would not have been a pleasant place to live beside had all the modern main road traffic still had to pass along it. Its ancient church of St Michael with its broached spire makes an interesting feature at the top of the village and this walking route begins close by and strikes west right across the broad acres of the limestone plateau to the next village of Chelmorton.

From the path to Chelmorton we get wide vistas across that stone-walled country to the south and west, an area thick with prehistoric burial sites. But it is the drystone walls erected after Enclosure Acts two centuries ago that take the eye and make us wonder at the hard industry undertaken in all weathers by armies of wall builders.

Chelmorton has its own attractive, spired church of St John the Baptist, also right at the top of the settlement and sheltered by tall trees and the steep, southern slopes of Chelmorton Low.

There's no better place to see the complex pattern of enclosing drystone walls in the White Peak than here behind the farms and cottages lining the main street of Chelmorton. Lanes and field paths allow a return to Taddington by way of the Townhead area of neighbouring Flagg village (well known for its point-to-point horse races every Easter) and then across Taddington Moor to the starting point with those wide plateau views behind you.

Level: ♥ ♥
Length: 5.5 miles (8.75 kms)
Ascent: 540 feet (165 metres)
Terrain: Exposed limestone plateau, mainly on paths with some walking on public lanes.
Park & Start: Taddington village. GR 141711
Info: Inns in Taddington and Chelmorton.

Five Wells
Chambered Cairn
Sough Top
A6
Pillwell Lane
morton
Moor Lane
Taddington
Flagg Lane
Flagg

Taddington and Chelmorton

① Starting near Taddington church take the footpath heading south-west and cross Slipperlow Lane.

② The path ahead crosses near the 1,437 feet (438 metres) summit of Sough Top before crossing Sough Lane then Pillwell Lane (this latter is part of the Pennine

Taddington from the south-east.

Bridleway) and continue in the same direction to come behind Chelmorton church at the top of its main street.

③ Walk straight down the main street, passing Townend Farm, then turn left along the lane to the first bend (to left).

The Hall, Flagg.

Five Wells chambered cairn, near Taddington.

Peter Dale, near Wormhill.

This part of the White Peak is richly endowed with relics from prehistory. The term "low" can be seen frequently on maps of the area and dates from Saxon times, denoting "a heaped structure". So most of the lows are associated with barrows or burial chambers.

4 Take the footpath ahead to soon cross Highstool Lane and so reach the Town Head corner of Flagg village.

One of the finest barrows in the district is Five Wells, constructed by New Stone Age immigrants and which lies at 1,400 feet (426 metres) a short distance to the north of the route described here, between Taddington and Chelmorton. It was explored by archaeologists at least twice in the nineteenth century and at least twelve skeletons, pottery and weapons were found. It was later used for burial purposes by Bronze Age inhabitants.

 Turn left on reaching the public lane and keep left round the bend then take the lane that aims north-east (on right) to cross Flagg Lane.

 Continue north-east along Whitefield Lane for 0.3 of a mile (0.5 km) to go along in the same direction on a field path that brings us to Moor Lane on Taddington Moor.

 Take Slipperlow Lane ahead to soon reach Taddington.

Taddington Dale from The Jarnett, Taddington.

At the heart of the White Peak, summer.

5 Sharp summits above the Upper Dove

A fairly short walk beneath the reef knolls below the source of the River Dove.

Only a short distance below its birth on the flanks of Axe Edge the River Dove enters its pastoral upper valley and is overlooked by several remarkably peak-like little hills. These are the remnants of reef knolls formed in a tropical sea in Carboniferous times. Walking routes can be worked

Level: ♥ ♥
Length: 4.5 miles (7.25 kms)
Ascent: 524 feet (160 metres)
Terrain: Field paths, lanes and steep hillside.
Park & Start: Earl Sterndale. GR 090670
Info: Inn at Earl Sterndale.

out to traverse the sharp crests of several of these, including conspicuous Parkhouse Hill and Chrome Hill, but the route described here gives gentler progress. We have close-up views of their slopes and the grasslands beside the meanderings of the young Dove that later in its progress southwards flows through several notable gorges including the famous Dovedale.

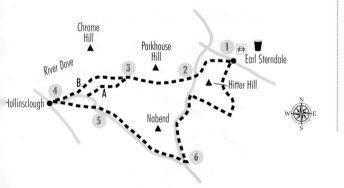

The Upper Dove Valley from Hitter Hill.

1 In Earl Sterndale village take the path that starts next to the Silent Woman Inn (notice her headless depiction!) and go west down the fields to Glutton Dale with fabulous views to the sharp profiles of Parkhouse Hill directly ahead.

2 Cross the road and continue on the path that skirts around the foot of Parkhouse Hill's south face and so reach the footbridge over the River Dove.

Earl Sterndale village lies not far from High Wheeldon, a hill gifted to the nation with a memorial on the summit to the men of Derbyshire and Staffordshire regiments killed in World War Two.

Parkhouse Hill (left) and Chrome Hill from above Glutton Dale.

Sharp summits above the Upper Dove

Chrome Hill from Parkhouse Hill.

3 Take either of two footpaths ahead, both of which soon come to the lane leading up to Hollinsclough village.

4 After looking at the various attractive buildings in this small settlement go back down the same lane a short distance then take the path to the right to reach the lane again at a sharp bend.

The village church at Earl Sterndale was attacked with German fire-bombs on the night of 9th November, 1941 and burnt out. Its ancient (maybe Saxon) font was split by the heat of the blaze. Everything, though, was eventually restored and re-dedicated in July, 1952.

Chrome Hill from Hollinsclough village.

Broadmeadow Hall from Pilsbury, Upper Dove Valley.

The apt motto of the Silent Woman Inn is "soft words turneth away wrath".

5 Go south-east along the lane, climbing steeply before reaching the junction with the road to Longnor (B5053).

6 Turn sharp left down the B5053, cross the River Dove again at Glutton Bridge and very soon turn right along the lane heading south-east. In less than 0.5 mile (0.75 km) take the footpath northwards that climbs up the eastern slope of Hitter Hill to reach Earl Sterndale again.

Sheen Hill from near Pilsbury.

6 Longstone Edge and Coombs Dale

Close up views of man's desecration of a grand limestone ridge.

Level: 🥾 🥾
Length: 5.75 miles (9.25 kms)
Ascent: 780 feet (238 metres)
Terrain: Steep path, ridge-top and dale-bottom tracks.
Park & Start: Calver crossroads. GR 239748
Info: Refreshments at Calver crossroads. Inn at Calver crossroads.

Longstone Edge is a 3.5 miles (5.5 kms) east-west backbone of limestone running from the banks of the River Derwent to the River Wye and rising to 1,280 feet (390 metres). It is a very conspicuous topographical feature of the White Peak. A walk along the eastern half of its length gives broad views to both north and south, and reveals the huge environmental damage that quarrying can inflict on upland landscapes. There's been an ongoing controversy about the continued quarrying on both the ridge-top and on both flanks. At last some effort is being made to restore some of the worst excavation eyesores.

Over a century ago one foot traveller along the crest of Longstone Edge described the sight of the top of Chatsworth's great conservatory glowing like a mirror (that building long since vanished from those gardens) and the heather and gorse covering the edge's western top. This contrast of vegetation between east and west still exists, though our route doesn't stray that far west.

The return is down the deep and sinuous Coombs Dale, cut into the northern side of Longstone Edge. The sheltering trees and restricted views make a pleasing contrast with the earlier ridge-top.

1 From the traffic lights at Calver crossroads walk a short way south up Hassop Road (B6001) and just above the garden centre a footpath on the right takes us up and round the flank of Calver Low.

2 Continue uphill on this path on the northern slopes of the grandly named Calver Peak to reach a meeting of several paths near the start of Deep Rake.

3 Now head due west on the track which keeps close to the deep trench (rake) which is now being back-filled and one day may look natural again!

Longstone Edge from Curbar Edge.

Longstone Edge from above Pilsley.

The village of Calver takes its name from the Old English words for "calf slope" – it lies on the west bank of the River Derwent, on sloping ground that soon steepens to form the eastern end of Longstone Edge.

(4) The long, narrow plantation to our left tends to hide Bleaklow Farm until you are right beside its gate. Simply continue along beside the trees with the great workings to the right. This section is called High Rake.

High Rake Quarry, Longstone Edge.

Quarrying activity on Longstone Edge.

5 Go down to the next junction of tracks then turn right and head due north across what is Longstone Moor for 0.75 mile (1.25 km) to the place called Black Harry Gate.

6 Turn right along the track to start the long, winding descent of Coombs Dale all the way to the Calver to Stoney Middleton road (A623), passing the old entrance to Sailet Hole Mine (fluorspar) on the right.

7 Turn right along the A623 the short distance back to the starting point at Calver crossroads.

Looking to Longstone Moor from Longstone Edge.

Close beside the old bridge over the Derwent stands the giant edifice of the former textile mill, built in 1785 and rebuilt after a fire in 1805. Production of cotton ceased in 1923 and subsequently it had various uses, including the production of glacé cherries using turnips and raspberry seeds to go in wartime jam using sawdust during World War Two! Later it was used as Colditz Castle in the television series and is now converted to luxury apartments.

Redway Wood and Longstone Edge.

Discovering Peakland's largest Pothole.

Level: 💙 💙
Length: 5 miles (8 kms)
Ascent: 500 feet (150 metres)
Terrain: Field paths and rough limestone hillside.
Park & Start: Peak Forest village. GR 114793
Info: Inn at Peak Forest.

The term "forest" was used in medieval times for a hunting ground, not necessarily dense woodland. The Royal Forest of the Peak covered a huge area where the Norman overlords hunted game. The present village of Peak Forest lies in a great bowl on the limestone plateau, its church one of the few dedicated to King Charles I. Little more than a mile to the north is the famous Eldon Hole, the largest pothole in the Peak District, on the slopes of Eldon Hill. At 1,541 feet (470 metres) this is actually the loftiest limestone hill in the National Park.

From the summit of Eldon Hill we get a tremendous view to the south, out across the limestone plateau towards Buxton and the fringing rim of gritstone moors beyond that. Turning to look north we see the nearer rim of Rushup Edge leading east to culminate in Mam Tor, "the shivering mountain" due to its unstable shales. In clear conditions this really is a good belvedere covering a goodly portion of the northernmost White Peak.

Our route turns east and south to complete the circuit, crossing a landscape pockmarked by long defunct, small scale quarrying and lead mining before reaching our starting point in Peak Forest.

1 From the crossroads near the church in Peak Forest take the lane heading north which is a section of the Pennine Bridleway, turning left at the first junction then, at Eldon Lane Farm, turn right.

2 After Sweetknoll Farm the lane becomes a footpath and almost immediately fork left to keep close to the drystone wall, aiming towards Eldon Hill straight ahead. All this ground is now Open Country.

Rushup Vale from Windy Knoll.

3 Eldon Hole can be seen as a dark scar on the slope ahead. Make directly towards it.

Eldon Hole was a notorious pothole in historical times. A goose that fell into the shaft maybe three centuries ago is reported to have emerged some days later at the mouth of Peak Cavern at Castleton two miles away with its plumage "singed by the fires of Hell"! So frightening was the sight of the pothole's mouth that quaint verse long ago challenged the passer-by to peep into the void "and keep his hair from lifting off his hat" – unless he is bald or has "sold his hair for more modish curls". Anyhow, take great care when viewing this abyss from its very brink.

Eldon Hole, near Peak Forest.

4 At Eldon Hole take care not to slip into the "bottomless" chasm. Then strike straight up the slope behind to reach the summit of Eldon Hill.

5 Just beyond this summit the northern side of the hill has been almost completely quarried away so take care when looking towards Rushup Edge. Turn to the east from the summit, heading towards the footpath coming up from Sweetknoll Farm and Peak Forest.

6 Turn left along this path to a junction of paths then turn right for 0.75 mile (1.25 km) to join the Limestone Way.

Paraglider on the slopes of Mam Tor.

About 1.5 miles (2.5 kms) north-east of the summit of Eldon Hill is the appropriately named Windy Knoll and here, in a deep fissure in the limestone, the great cave hunter Sir William Boyd Dawkins and Rooke Pennington found 6,800 prehistoric animal bones – the greatest number found in so modest an area. It must have been a drinking hole visited by bison, reindeer and various deer species. This discovery convinced Boyd Dawkins that at one time there must have been a huge seasonal movement of such animals through the Winnats Pass, which lies between Windy Knoll and Castleton to the east.

7 Turn right along the Limestone Way to head south, back towards Peak Forest. In half a mile (0.8 km) fork right off the Limestone Way on a path that soon runs beside the long plantation along Oxlow Rake.

8 At the end of the plantation turn left down to Old Dam Lane where we turn right along it and at the road junction turn left down to the centre of Peak Forest.

Suffolk rams near Peak Forest.

Limestone plateau near Green Fairfield.

Near Peak Forest.

8 Villages at the limestone edge

Sheen, Warslow and up on Revidge.

Level: 🐾 🐾
Length: 8.5 miles (13.5 kms)
Ascent: 755 feet (230 metres)
Terrain: Field paths and steep lanes.
Park & Start: Sheen village. GR 113615
Info: Inns at Sheen, Warslow and Reaps Moor

A singularly attractive corner of the Staffordshire Moorlands is that middle reach of the Manifold Valley a short distance below the high gritstone moors at the river's birth upon Axe Edge. It is a broad, green valley crossed by the meandering Manifold — typical mixed and dairy farming territory. Our route starts out at the tree-lined, ridge-top linear village of Sheen and crosses the grasslands to climb the western slopes to reach the hillside settlement of Warslow. A large part of this area once formed part of the giant Harpur Crewe estate and now much of it is owned by the Peak District National Park.

A climb out of Warslow to the west brings us off the underlying Carboniferous limestone and onto the younger gritstone high ground; here is a darker landscape with heather moor atop Revidge and fabulous views to every point of the compass. As is often the case mid-height hills provide the best balanced vistas and this one from Revidge at 1,312 feet (400 metres) is no exception.

Swinging round to the north we complete the circuit by way of Reaps Moor and across the southern slopes of Sheen Hill to our starting point near the conspicuous copper spire of St Luke's parish church at Sheen.

1 From Sheen parish church walk south along the road a very short way and take the second footpath to the right, close to a field barn.

2 Walk due west down several fields and soon come down a narrow track to New House Farm at Brund hamlet. Turn right down the lane and walk to the first junction.

3 Turn left to pass close beside the former Brund mill (now a dwelling) and cross the bridge over the River Manifold.

4 In a few hundred metres take the field path on the left and cross diagonally to join the lane near Hulme House Farm.

Looking over Ecton and the Manifold Valley from Ecton Hill.

Sheen parish church in spring.

5 Turn left along the lane past the first cottage (on right) and take the path just beyond that slants up right across five fields (lots of rushes) to cross Hayesgate Lane.

6 Cross the next level field and so down to the tiny stream, keeping on the approximately straight line to soon reach the last large field — usually boggy in the middle — and aim for the top left corner against the wood. Here a flight of stone steps brings you to the Longnor to Warslow road (B5053).

7 Turn left and soon pass the gates of Warslow Hall, then pass between a pair of pretty ponds before climbing to the junction with the road to Hartington. Continue straight ahead to reach Warslow in another third of a mile (0.5 km).

The ridge-top village of Sheen is a true linear settlement with most of its dwellings clinging to the road that runs north – south. It is saved from being the bleak, wind-blasted place it could have been by the wealth of planted trees that cluster about the church and neighbouring buildings which are a legacy from the days of Alexander Beresford Hope in the middle of the nineteenth century.

An old church at Sheen was replaced in 1852 by a remarkable new one designed by the great Victorian architect William Butterfield (1814–1900), the Gothic revivalist and high churchman. Its blunt, copper spire is conspicuous for miles around. Adjacent is what was known as The Palace, really one of the grandest vicarages in this part of England and later sold off as a private house.

The Palace, Sheen.

8   Turn right at the road junction and go up through the village to the top of the hill — about 0.75 of a mile (1.25 kms) then take the footpath on the right to cross rough pasture, then the remains of a patchy plantation and so enter Open Country. We soon gain the highest point of the track with a good stand of conifers on the left.

Ruined barn near Warslow.

9   To reach the actual top of Revidge turn up left through the trees, cross the heather and soon gain the trig. pillar at 1,312 feet (400 metres) for the fabulous 360 degree view.

Neva Cottage, Warslow.

10 Return to the track and turn left (north) to continue past Cuckoostone Farm to the public road. Go along northwards to pass through this district of Reaps Moor (Butcher's Arms Inn) and down to the quaint church of St John (left). Here we turn right along a lane that soon crosses the Longnor road at a furniture factory and so down to the first sharp, right corner.

11 Fork left, cross the bridge over a stream and take the footpath on the right to meander across level fields before crossing the River Manifold on a footbridge and go straight up a narrow track between high hedges to the lane close to Ridge End Farm. Turn right and in about 0.5 of a mile (0.8 km) go over the crossroads with the southern slopes of Sheen Hill to the left.

12 Follow this lane and it soon climbs steeply before reaching Manor Farm at Sheen. Turn right to return to the parish church and the starting point.

The lower pond, Warslow Hall.

9 Parsley Hay, Pilsbury Castle and Carder Low

A flavour of Derbyshire's share of the limestone plateau.

The River Dove forms the boundary between Derbyshire and Staffordshire throughout its length and this particular circular route covers a small area of Derbyshire between the Dove and the High Peak Trail.

This latter forms part of the Pennine Bridleway. It follows the trackbed of the former Buxton to Ashbourne railway constructed by the LNWR and only operational between 1899 and 1963. From the site of the former Parsley Hay station on this line our route crosses typical stone-walled farmland to reach the enigmatic site of Pilsbury Castle overlooking the east bank of the Dove. Wandering south on a lane parallel with the river we come close to Ludwell Farm, its name derived from the Old English words "hlud" and "waella" — literally "loud spring" which must

Level: 🐾 🐾
Length: 6 miles (9.5 kms)
Ascent: 500 feet (150 metres)
Terrain: Field paths and lanes. One stiff climb.
Park & Start: Parsley Hay. GR 148636
Info: Nearest refreshments at Hartington. GR 128604.

refer to the nearby hillside spring that still exists.

A zigzag climb up the eastern slope of the valley brings us to Open Country upon Carder Low, maybe named after the medieval Richard Carder — "Carder's hill". If we go up to the actual top of this eminence at 1,246 feet (380 metres) there are wonderful, wide views across the Dove Valley into the Staffordshire Moorlands.

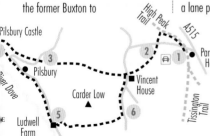

1　From the car park at former Parsley Hay railway station beside the Ashbourne to Buxton road (A515) walk north along the High Peak Trail (also serving as the Pennine Bridleway). In less than .3 of a mile (.5 km) turn left down the path that crosses from Moscar Farm.

2　Soon cross the lane at Darley Farm and continue across the fields to Vincent House. Cross the lane here and follow the field path west, passing the unusual (for limestone country) pond that serves four fields. Continue due west.

3　Cross the next narrow lane and keep to the path as it heads north-west and drops to the unusual site of Pilsbury Castle mounds overlooking the Dove.

A White Peak sheep sale, Biggin by Hartington.

Pilsbury Castle beside the River Dove is something of a mystery. Right through the golden age of Victorian archaeological excavation no-one seems to have investigated this site fully. Recent opinion is that it was an Iron Age fortress and a focal settlement for the Upper Dove district. At a later time it was chosen by the Normans as a castle site founded about 1100 as a command post for what must have been hostile country. Maybe the inhabitants moved away to more fertile lowland and Pilsbury slowly decayed, leaving the enigmatic, grassy ramparts we see today. Whatever the truth it's an enchanting place.

Pilsbury Castle mounds, Upper Dove Valley.

(4) Turn back south along the track to soon reach Pilsbury, a hamlet of farms. Continue south on the public lane, passing Parks Barn.

(5) About .75 of a mile (1.25 km) beyond Parks Barn we approach Ludwell Farm. Turn up the steep, zigzag path to the left and climb onto the flank of Carder Low (Open Country). This path continues fairly directly to reach the public lane that comes up from Hartington.

Farm sale at Pilsbury Grange.

6 Turn left along the lane to get back to Vincent House and simply follow the path to the right, back to the High Peak Trail and Parsley Hay.

The old cart, Pilsbury looking to Sheen Hill.

The large pool passed on this walk between Parsley Hay and Pilsbury is most unusual for the limestone plateau of the White Peak. Quite a considerable area must have been surfaced by a layer of impervious clay so that run-off water largely from rainfall collected here. Adjacent landowners must have decided to share this useful water resource during the period of the Enclosure Acts and built the drystone walls to give several farmers access to it for their summering cattle.

10 Wetton and Thor's Cave

Visiting one of the great natural and archaeological wonders of the White Peak.

Level: 🥾 🥾
Length: 3.5 miles (5.5 kms)
Ascent: 400 feet (120 metres)
Terrain: Steep field paths, a rocky scramble and level railway trackbed.
Park & Start: Wetton village. GR 109552
Info: Inn at Wetton.

Standing high on the limestone plateau between the deep valleys of the Dove and the Manifold the little stone village of Wetton has a medieval church largely rebuilt in 1820 and so contains the royal arms of George IV. It makes a

good starting point for a short circular walk that takes in the most dramatic part of the Manifold Valley.

A worthwhile short detour allows the thrill of seeing Thor's Cave at close quarters. The climb to the entrance gives the impression of an approach to a cathedral door, opened wide and dark inside.

In complete contrast the walk south along the trackbed of the former Leek and Manifold Light Railway (now the Manifold Way) makes for easy, level strolling. Imagine travelling on the delightful narrow-gauge trains between 1904 and 1934; for all the world it had

the feel of an Indian hill railway because it was modelled on the Barsi Light Railway. Where the railway turned south up the valley of the River Hamps we cross the Manifold for the steep ascent near the great limestone crag of Beeston Tor, to whose cave Saint Bertram is supposed to have retreated. That climb brings us back, by field path and lane to hilltop Wetton.

1 From the car park at the southern edge of Wetton take the path north-west up one paddock and turn left along a lane out of the village, soon beginning to descend towards the Manifold Valley.

2 From the junction of lanes at the edge of the village follow the footpath heading west down several fields with the back of the great crag containing Thor's Cave ahead.

3 Instead of dropping into the wooded valley keep left on a traversing path to the left and soon come round to face the great mouth of Thor's Cave. Climb up to get a close view of the cave entrance and of the view down into the valley.

Store cattle near Wetton.

The Manifold Valley is the most highly concentrated area for archaeological caves in the entire Peak District.

(4) Take care on the steep path down through the wood to reach the valley floor. Cross the river on the footbridge.

(5) Turn left and follow the trackbed of the former railway (now the Manifold Way) for almost 1.5 miles (2.5 kms) to the mouth of the Hamps Valley that comes in on the right side.

Beeston Tor and the dry bed of the River Manifold.

Thor's Cave is the great natural sight of the Manifold. It is important, too, as an archaeological site. Samuel Carrington, schoolmaster at Wetton, and others did the first serious investigations and discovered pottery, iron objects and a Roman coin in 1864. A decade later the great geologist W. Boyd Dawkins did work here and in 1935 the Rev. G.H.Wilson discovered a rich store of lion, hyena, wolf, hippopotamus and other animal bones of inter-glacial times in the small Elderbush Cave adjacent to Thor's Cave. This smaller cave has been described as "one of the most important archaeological sites in this part of England".

The Manifold Light Railway was opened to traffic on 27 June, 1904 with carriages of open saloon type but the line's main purpose was to convey milk from producing farms to dairies farther afield, and to carry coal and grain to the farms and villages on the surrounding hillsides. Some of the curves on this narrow gauge line were so tight that it was said "a driver was able to see the nape of his own neck". Times were hard in the thirties and the line was closed on 28th September, 1934 but there is a newly opened information centre and café at the original northern terminus at Hulme End, between Hartington and Warslow.

6 Cross the River Manifold close to Beeston Tor which is conspicuous ahead.

7 Now climb steeply up to Larkstone Lane, cross it to continue up to Carr Lane and soon take another path on the left that crosses the fields at an easy gradient back to Wetton.

Grindon church and buttercup meadow.

Washday, Grindon.